Language and Literacy Supports for Struggling Readers:

Meeting the Goals of No Child Left Behind

Renitta Goldman
Jerry Aldridge
Kelly A. Russell

Publication of this resource is supported by the Division of Personnel Preparation, Office of Special Education Programs and Rehabilitative Services, U. S. Department of Education (Contract No.
HE325E02047) and the University of Alabama at Birmingham. The
information and points of view expressed in this document do not
necessarily reflect the opinions of the funding agency.

Library of Congress Control Number: 2007925683

ISBN 1-59421-033-0

Published by Seacoast Publishing, Inc.

TABLE OF CONTENTS

INTRODUCTION

The following text is designed as a resource for teaching struggling readers from grades preK-12. Publication of this resource is supported by the Division of Personnel Preparation, Office of Special Education Programs and Rehabilitative Services, U. S. Department of Education (Contract No. HE325E02047) and the University of Alabama at Birmingham. The information and points of view expressed in this document do not necessarily reflect the opinions of the funding agency.

Students enrolled in a federally funded masters degree program known as Project TEACH: Teachers as Advocates for Children of Diverse Heritage participated and contributed in the implementation of the included ideas and strategies in their classrooms. The graduate students completed a Master of Arts degree in Education in a collaborative teacher program. This was formerly known as special education. Since in the 21st century a large portion of literacy instruction for struggling readers occurs in the regular classroom with support from collaborative teachers, it was considered essential that their training include more experiences in literacy, including language development.

This text is designed to help teachers plan, implement, and modify instruction for those students needing additional support in oral language development as well as reading and writing. Although all children would benefit from this material, struggling readers will particularly gain from these strategies and activities. We hope the following ideas will make a positive impact on the language and literacy development of struggling readers.

Modifications of regular education language and literacy instruction are now more vital than ever for the success of struggling readers. Specifically, the *No Child Left Behind Act* of 2001 has influenced how assessment takes place. Students identified under the Individuals with Disabilities Education Act (IDEA) are required to participate in regular education testing. In order for these students to succeed, it is necessary for teachers to know and apply appropriate modifications in language and literacy instruction.

Finally, most of the ideas that were published in the book *Teaching Children to Read* (Goldman, Aldridge, & Worthington, 2003) have been included in this resource. We hope this resource will help you become a transformative teacher for all children, but especially your struggling readers.

Renitta Goldman, Professor
University of Alabama at Birmingham

Jerry Aldridge, Professor
University of Alabama at Birmingham

Kelly A. Russell, Teaching and Research Assistant
University of Alabama at Birmingham

CHAPTER ONE

Struggling Readers and the Goals of No Child Left Behind

Who Are Struggling Readers?

In many ways, we have made great strides in understanding struggling readers during the past 30 years. In other ways, we have not. We have come a long way in determining who struggling readers are since the publication of *Teaching Reading to Slow and Disabled Learners* (Kirk, Kliebhan, & Lerner, 1978). Kirk and his colleagues spent an entire chapter defining "slow and disabled readers." There were so many types of struggling readers in this chapter, it was enough to make teachers leave the profession. There were all types of intellectually challenged children that included slow learners, borderline, mildly retarded, moderately retarded, not to mention the disabled learner. Then, there were all sorts of reasons for failure, including neurological dysfunction, cerebral dominance issues, visual defects, hereditary and genetic defects, cultural differences, language differences, emotional and social problems, not to mention problems with auditory perception, sound blending, auditory closure, speed of visual perception, visual memory issues, and finally an entire group of language disorders.

On the opposite end of the spectrum, Richard Allington's *What Really Matters for Struggling Readers'* first edition was published in 2001. This resource provides a wealth of ideas about what struggling readers need. However, it does not go into any detail as to what a struggling reader is.

For purposes of this book, a struggling reader is defined as any child who does not meet the assessment standards of the prescribed instruments used by the State in which the child lives to meet the requirements of the No Child Left Behind Law. Of course, there is much more to struggling readers than test scores. Every child is far more than any of his test scores. However, the purpose of this book is to help struggling readers meet the goals of No Child Left Behind and for the **purposes of this book only** we use the definition of a struggling reader in relationship to the law.

Having said this, there are two salient points we would like to make. First, we use the term "struggling reader" because it is used in the current literature. We realize that since the reauthorization of Individuals with Disabilities Education Act (I.D.E.A.) in the early 1990s the politically correct terminology always begins with children or people first. For example, instead of the learning disabled child, we now refer to her as a child with a learning disability. The second and most important point we would like to make is that struggling readers are often not seen as individual children. We believe every child has some incredible gifts or individual abilities that are important to find, value, and develop. This cannot be done if we see the child as only a notch on the curriculum standards or assessment continuum. We make a terrible mistake if we think that we are "individualizing" instruction when we are only trying to help the child meet the standards. We encourage you to move beyond the pages of this book and see each child's unique potential and work to develop it. Think about it.

Finding a child's unique potential has become less and less common because we spend all of our time trying to meet the standards. However, the focus of this book is helping struggling readers meet the standards. We hope you will work hard to move beyond just meeting the standards and truly see each child as someone who is far more than a test taker.

What Does No Child Left Behind Say About Reading Instruction?

There is a wealth of information concerning federal guidelines and reading instruction. The most basic information we can provide is the fact that the No Child Left Behind (NCLB) legislation was signed into law in early 2002. It was highly influenced by the findings of the National Reading Panel's 2000 report found in Teaching Children To Read. "To assist schools in meeting the reading requirements of NCLB, the federal government added two new initiatives as a part of the legislation: the Early Reading First initiative for children ages 3-5 years and the Reading First initiative for children in kindergarten through third grade" (Kirkland, Aldridge, & Kuby, 2007, p. ix). The Early Reading First Goals included:
- Oral Language
- Phonological Awareness
- Print Awareness
- Alphabetic Knowledge

The Reading First goals were:
- Phonemic Awareness
- Phonics
- Vocabulary
- Comprehension

For a more comprehensive explanation of Early Reading First and Reading First, we recommend *No Child Left Behind: A Desktop Reference* (2002). Please note that by the time a reader has been determined to be a struggling one, he is most likely somewhere between kindergarten and third grade, the age in which the Reading First goals are used. Why is this important? Struggling readers may still have trouble with many of the Early Reading First goals. The following Chapters will address most of the Early Reading First goals as well as the Reading First goals.

The Challenge

Currently, only a small percentage of children are exempt from testing requirements of No Child Left Behind. That means numerous struggling readers must take standardized tests annually with no modifications. For example, we are familiar with a fourth grade child who has severe cerebral palsy. She cannot hold a writing device and cannot focus her attention on a paper or book in the traditional ways that other children can. For the past two years, she has been required to take the same tests as her classmates without any accommodations or modifications.

Struggling readers all over the United States and its territories are in the same boat. They need extra instructional support in attempting to meet the goals of No Child Left Behind. The following chapters are designed to provide some of this support through meaningful instructional strategies. But first, chapters two, three, and four are designed to answer important questions about language and reading. Chapter Two is concerned with "What is oral language?" and "What is reading and writing?" and Chapter Three considers, "What is readiness?"

REFERENCES

Allington, R.L., (2001) *What really matters for struggling readers: Designing research-based programs.* New York: Addison-Wesley/Longman.

Kirk, S.A. , Kliebhan, J.M., & Lerner, J.W. (1978). *Teaching reading to slow and disabled learners.* Boston: Houghton Mifflen.

Kirkland, L., Aldridge, J., & Kuby, P. (2007). *Integrating environmental print across the curriculum pre-K – 3: Making instruction meaningful.* Thousand Oaks, CA: Corwin Press.

National Institute of Child Health and Human Development (2000). *Report of the National Reading Panel. Teaching children to read: An evidence-based assessment of the scientific research literature on reading and its implications for reading instruction* (NIH Publication No. 00-4769). Washington, DC: U.S. Government Printing Office.

CHAPTER TWO

What is oral language development, reading, and writing?

What is oral language development?

Oral language development provides the rich and needed foundation for reading and writing. Teaching reading and writing, without considering language development is like trying to drive a car without gasoline. Oral language development is the fuel that is necessary for reading and writing. In order to understand language development, it is a good idea to put it in the context of other related terms. Communication and speech surround and support language development, but they are not the same as language development.

Communication has two broad definitions. First, communication is the umbrella under which both **speech** and **language** fall. A second definition of communication is the transmission of a message, with or without language. For example, when a cat is perched in a tree looking down at a dog, it is transmitting the message, "I see you. You can't bother me. I'm in the tree." However, this message is transmitted without speech or language.

Speech is defined as the mechanical part of communication. In street terms, it is the vocalizing, or "moving of your mouth". Struggling readers may have trouble producing some of the sounds of their primary language, but this is not the same thing as language.

So what is language? For purposes of this book, language is defined as communication that involves a series of words that are intended to convey a meaningful message. The order of these words is known as **syntax**. Correct syntax varies from language to language. For example, in English, in the simplest of terms, we use subject-verb-object. We say, "I go to town." In Japanese, the syntax is different. A Japanese speaker would put the verb last and say the equivalent of "I town go." The syntax in Japanese is subject-object-verb. Syntax is important to language development, but it is not the only thing that makes up language. Language also consists of **semantics** and **pragmatics**.

Semantics has to do with the meaning system of language. When we say "good-bye," it usually means that someone is leaving. **Pragmatics** is concerned with social interaction. In a sense, it is the "manners" of language. We say "please" when we are asking for something, and "thank you" when we receive something.

Every language also has a "sound system" which is sometimes referred to as **phonology**. Producing these sounds would be in the realm of **speech**, but the order in which they are used to convey a meaningful message would be considered **language**. So our "sound system" is important to both language and speech.

Remember, oral language development is the foundation for reading and writing, and many of our struggling readers have limited experiences in the development of oral language. Parents who continually interact with and read to their children enhance their children's oral language development (Barton, 2004). "In-depth observational studies over a substantial period of time by Har and Risley (1995) recorded the interactions of parents with their children – both type and frequency. The researchers reached a startling conclusion: Three-year-old children in professional families had a vocabulary as large of that of the *parents* in the study who were on welfare" (Barton, 2004, p. 10).

The salience of oral language development to reading and writing cannot be overstated. However, as we can see, many struggling readers enter school with limited oral language development. Further, some have had limited preschool experiences. The issue of oral language development is then exacerbated when they enter kindergarten or first grade because the focus of reading instruction under No Child Left Behind is more on phonemic awareness, phonics, vocabulary, fluency, and comprehension as they relate to reading and writing. Oral language development is not emphasized, and because of this, it is often left out of consideration in curriculum decisions. In Chapter 5 we provide several suggestions for enhancing the oral language development of struggling readers.

In order to teach reading and writing to struggling readers, it is necessary to determine just what reading and writing are. One way to examine this is to determine who in the following family can read and who cannot.

The Wilcox Family

Mrs. Wilcox says she cannot read. She clips coupons from the newspaper and the weekly flyers she gets in the mail to use in purchasing products when she shops. However, Mrs. Wilcox is not able to help her fourth grade son Robert with his homework that requires reading. Does Mrs. Wilcox read?

Mr. Wilcox works as a plumber. He travels from house to house as a part of his job. One day he arrives at the Davis' house while they are out and finds a note that says, "The sink in the kitchen is broken. The toilets you fixed last week are working just fine. Please just fix the sink." Mr. Wilcox proceeds to the kitchen and begins working. But, like Mrs. Wilcox, he cannot read well enough to help Robert with his homework.

Robert, the fourth grade son, wants to be a botanist and identifies plants in the neighborhood as a hobby. Every time he finds a new one, he goes home and looks it up in a plant identification book. He also enjoys reading adolescent novels.

Kara is Mr. and Mrs. Wilcox's daughter who is in first grade. She can identify all of the 44 sounds in the English language and knows most of the 220 words found on the old Dolch Sight Word List. When Kara "reads" a book that her teacher has sent home, she can pronounce every word correctly but does not have any ideas about what the story is about. Can Kara read?

Most people agree that Robert is a reader, and many believe that Mr. Wilcox is too. After all, he was able to read the note left by the Davis family and knows where to begin his job, but what about Mrs. Wilcox and Kara? Are they readers? Do they read? That depends on what definition we use. To determine if Mrs. Wilcox and Kara can read, let's consider definitions of reading and then return to the Wilcox family.

What is Reading?

When Project TEACH students took their first literacy class in the program, they were asked to determine the definition of reading. While students were able to formulate definitions, at first they could not agree on what reading is (Goldman & Aldridge, 2003). Most reading experts define reading as getting meaning from print. Without meaning there would be no comprehension, and without comprehension there would be no reading (Cunningham & Allington, 2003). Reading also involves bringing meaning to print. Our prior knowledge on a subject makes a big difference in whether or not we are able to comprehend a printed message. If someone is reading about a volcano and has never seen one, then there is limited prior knowledge brought to print. However, if a person lives near a volcano in Hawaii or Italy, then that person's experience with volcanoes or prior knowledge makes a difference. The person might visualize a nearby volcano or remember a grandparent telling a story about an active volcano.

Prior knowledge is quite important to meaning. For example, if a standardized test has an item in which the examinee is to identify a "toboggan," the person being tested will be influenced by prior knowledge. If the individual is from the Northern United States, chances are that person will know a toboggan is a sled. However, if they are from the Southern United States, a toboggan is a hat.

What is Literacy?

L iteracy is a term more often used than reading in the 21st century. What is literacy? Literacy is both reading and writing. Many years ago teachers thought we had to learn to read first and then we would learn to write later. Today we know that students learn to read better by writing, and they learn to write better by reading. Reading and writing go together. Taken together, reading and writing are called literacy.

In general terms, there are three types of literacy. These are: 1) functional literacy, 2) cultural literacy, and 3) critical literacy. *Functional literacy* can be defined as "walking around" literacy. Functional literacy is being able to read and write just enough to stay out of trouble. Functional literacy includes recognizing the correct restroom sign (male or female), identifying basic environmental print such as stop signs, fast food restaurants, canned food labels, billboards, and other simple print found in the environment that most people encounter every day.

Cultural literacy is the reading and writing taught in schools. As such, there are two types of cultural literacy. These include *mainstream cultural literacy*. This is what is traditionally taught in schools. For example, "Columbus discovered America." In the past, this was a fact taught in most schools in the United States. There is also *marginalized cultural literacy*, which is defined as the stories and readings that have not been traditionally taught in schools. Examples of marginalized cultural literacy include women's stories, Native American perspectives, and other information that has not been emphasized in schools.

Finally, and most importantly, there is *critical literacy*. Critical literacy is defined as teaching children to read and write with a skeptical eye or teaching students to question everything they read. Who said that? What perspective is being presented? What are other points of view? Ultimately, the goal of literacy instruction is to critical literacy, but most students with special needs are never taught this because many teachers believe that as long as students are working on functional or cultural literacy, there is no room for critical literacy. Hopefully, this resource will help teachers correct this misconception.

In more specific terms, there are other types of literacy that are necessary for success in the 21st century. These include *information literacy, communications literacy, technological literacy,* and *media literacy* just to mention a few. Information literacy requires the ability to sort through the information overload and determine what is important. The skill of interpretation is also needed. When students are confronted with conflicting or diverse viewpoints, how do they go about determining what is accurate? Information literacy is often necessary for critical literacy.

Communications literacy includes new forms of literacy necessary for telecomputing. For example, students now must learn how to communicate through email and practice email etiquette, known as *netiquette* and appropriate forms of communicating through email. New forms of communication are developing rapidly, and this requires *communications literacy*.

Technological literacy involves the use of computers and machines. Word processing and the many other ways of using a computer as a tool are forms of *technological literacy*.

Finally, *media literacy* goes beyond reading and writing to encoding and analyzing the numerous messages with which we are bombarded through everything from television commercials to the movies we see. Evaluating these messages is another important form of literacy.

Returning to the Wilcox Family

So who in the Wilcox family can read? By the definitions we have used – getting meaning from print and bringing meaning to print – everyone in the family can read with the exception of Kara. Mr. Wilcox constructed meaning from the Davis' family note. Robert gets meaning by finding the plants he sees throughout the neighborhood in his botany book. Even Mrs. Wilcox can read by our definition. Granted, it is only at the *functional* level, but she can get meaning from coupons and then use them at the store.

Kara, however, by our definition cannot read. She knows her sounds and many words but does not comprehend them. This presents a major problem when we consider the implied definition of reading used in *No Child Left Behind*. The National Institute for Child Health and Human Development (NICHD) and the Secretary of Education were charged by Congress to select a group of scientists in reading research to serve as a part of the National Reading Panel. Most of these scientists chose a skills-based approach to reading (Yatvin, 2002). Using a skills-based definition of reading, reading can be defined as an understanding of the sounds of the English language and word recognition. According to a skills-based definition, Kara can read. Chances are, Kara is being taught by a skills-based phonics program in the first grade, and the focus on comprehension or meaning from print will come later in her reading instruction.

So who in the Wilcox family can read? If we are more inclusive of the definition used by reading experts and also include the definition implied by the National Reading Panel and the *No Child Left Behind* legislation, we can see every member of the Wilcox family as at least *potential* readers.

Why is this important? In inclusive classrooms of today it is necessary for both regular and special education teachers to see each child as a *potential* reader. By whatever definition we might choose for reading or literacy, each student has the right to appropriate instruction. Students should be taught *both* the skills necessary for literacy as well as meaning or how to make sense out of what they read. In this book we take a both/and approach instead of an either/or focus with literacy. Both phonics and meaning are necessary for reading. All students are potential readers and deserve comprehensive, systematic instruction to ultimately achieve critical literacy.

The Cueing Systems of Reading

I n order to develop a comprehensive, systematic reading program, we must teach students to use all of the cueing systems necessary for reading. We often ask our college students, "What did your teacher or parent tell you to do when you were a child when you couldn't figure out a word?" The answer is always, "sound it out." That is just one of the four ways to figure out the word. There are three others. When we read, we can use the *graphophonic, syntactic, semantic,* or the *pragmatic* cueing systems to determine a word.

When our teacher or parents said "sound it out", they were asking us to rely on the *graphophonic* cueing system. This involves the knowledge and use of written sounds .

The *syntactic cueing system* can also be used. This has to do with grammar and word. Order. What part of speech is this word? For example, in English we learn that an adjective usually comes before the noun. We may read "She lives in a brick house." In English we would not find, "She lives in a house brick."

Another way to figure out a word is by using the *semantic cueing system*. This has to do with meaning. What word makes sense? In the sentence, "I am going to the st__", what word "makes sense?" We know that the "store" would make sense, but not start, stop, or stars.

Then there is the *pragmatic cueing system*. This has to do with determining a word through culture or context. Earlier we mentioned that in the Northern United States the word "toboggan" would mean sled. In the Southern United States the term means a hat. If we are reading about people who are dressing to stay warm, we can figure out that toboggan would mean a hat.

Conclusions

Every student is a potential reader and writer. Some may only develop functional literacy, but most have the potential to move all the way to critical literacy. Every child has the right to comprehensive, systematic reading instruction. We must use definitions of methods of reading and writing that include all students. As good teachers, we must not neglect teaching phonics and word recognition, but we must also not neglect teaching comprehension. What does this mean for children who are just beginning to read and write – both those who are in early childhood education and those who have already failed by traditional methods of teaching reading and writing?

In Chapter Two we will examine both what is readiness and how to teach reading and writing to those who have failed by traditional methods as well as those who are not yet ready for formal literacy instruction.

REFERENCES

Barton, P.E. (2004). Why does the gap persist? *Educational Leadership*, (62)3, 9-13.

Cunningham, P.M., & Allington, R.L. (2003). *Classrooms that work: They can all read and write* (3rd ed.). Boston: Allyn and Bacon.

Goldman, R., Aldridge, J., & Worthington, L. (in press). Improving literacy instruction of special education teachers through additional course work and support. *Journal of Instructional Psychology*.

Hart, B., & Risley, T.R. (1995) *Meaningful differences in the everyday experiences of young American children*. Baltimore, MD: Paul H. Brookes.

U.S. Department of Education, Office of Elementary and Secondary Education, *No Child Left Behind: A Desktop Reference*, Washington, DC, 2002.

Yatvin, J. (2002). Babes in the woods: The wanderings of the National Reading Panel. *Phi Delta Kappan*, 83(5), 364-368.

CHAPTER THREE

What is Readiness? – Teaching Reading and Writing from the Start

One of the big buzz words in education today is the term "readiness". Just exactly what is *readiness*? As we discussed in Chapter One, the definition we choose of readiness is salient to how we teach. Similarly, the definition of *readiness* is also important to how we determine which children are ready for what types of instruction in reading and writing.

What is Readiness?

Readiness has many definitions, but it may be helpful to define readiness related to reading and writing using three related terms: 1) *developmental readiness*, 2) *reading readiness,* and 3) *emergent literacy*.

Developmental readiness refers to all of the physical or physiological components necessary for readiness – that is, the determinants necessary for a child to focus on print. For example, unless the child is visually impaired and will need to read using other means, the child must focus her eyes before she is ready to read. The child must be able to have a certain attention span before she is able to focus on reading. These physical developments are necessary *developmental readiness* for reading. Most infants are not ready to read and write because they lack the *developmental readiness* necessary for formal reading.

Reading readiness is defined as "reading in the beginning stages" or what was defined in Chapter One as *functional literacy*. If we include functional reading in the definition of reading, then reading readiness would involve reading in the beginning stages. Most two to three-year-olds recognize the golden arches as they pass McDonald's. If we use environmental print to teach reading, then we do not have to get children ready to read. We can use their abilities to read in the beginning stages to help move them toward cultural literacy (Aldridge, Kirkland, and Kuby, 2002).

Emergent literacy can be defined as children who begin reading and writing because they have been immersed in a print rich environment. Their parents or guardians read to them. These children see print everywhere and see adults and children engaged in all types of literacy activities. While emergent literacy may occur in some children, most teachers have seen children who could be "drowned" in print, and they would still not learn to read and write. Literacy is social knowledge, and some direct, explicit instruction is necessary to ensure that children learn to read and write.

What Does it Take to Get a Child Ready to Read and Write?

From the early to mid 1900s reading experts believed a child must have a mental age of 6 1/2 years in order to be able to learn to read and write (Morphett & Washburne, 1931). Today we know that this is not true (Aldridge, Kirkland, and Kuby, 2002). Until recently some early childhood educators used visual discrimination, visual memory, auditory discrimination, and other similar activities with the idea that they were getting children ready to read. For example, they would have children complete worksheets in which they had to find a triangle that looked like another triangle. While these activities were probably harmless, they *did not* get children ready to read. In order for children to read even at the beginning, five essential elements are required. In order for children to learn to read, instruction must involve several things:

1) including letters and words,
2) using them in some meaningful context,
3) taking into account the prior knowledge of the students,
4) involving authentic or "real world" activities, and
5) making direct connections back to print.

Looking at shapes or listening to sounds in isolation does not meet these five requirements. In other words, visual memory or auditory discrimination activities do not teach children to read.

Where Do We Begin at the Beginning?

There are several appropriate ways to teach children to read and write. Some of the best ways to teach beginning readers and writers are though the following: Using environmental print, the key vocabulary approach, labeling objects, Daily News, the beginnings of the writing process, using shared reading experiences, using ideas from Reading Recovery, and teaching the alphabet in context.

➤**Environmental Print.**

Environmental print is defined as "print found in the natural environment of the child. This would include logos, labels, road signs, billboards, and other print found in the child's immediate ecology" (Kirkland, Aldridge, & Kuby, 1991, p. 219). Environmental print is an important tool because children see it everywhere, and we can use it to help them learn letters, sounds, and words (Aldridge, Kirkland, & Kuby, 2002).

Environmental print has many benefits for teaching reading and writing at the beginning stage. Children see themselves as readers and writers when environmental print is used for instruction, and young children actively seek out print found in their environment (Aldridge & Rust, 1987). It also bridges the gap between school and home (Aldridge, Kirkland, & Kuby, 2002).

The instructional value of environmental print is related to helping children translate what they see though environmental print into standard manuscript or computer generated print. Helping children make grocery lists or lists of their favorite restaurants helps them construct the idea that what I see in my environment I can write down. (For specific suggestions on how to teach environmental print, see Aldridge, Kirkland, & Kuby, 2002).

➤**The Key Vocabulary Approach.**

Another approach for beginning readers is *Key Words* or the *Key Vocabulary Approach* (Veatch, Sawicki, Elliot, Barnett, & Blakey, 1973). The following steps are used in implementing this approach.

Step one. The teacher elicits a word from every child, every day. All words are accepted. For example, the teacher my prompt by saying "What is the scariest word you can think of?" etc.

Step two. The teacher prints the word on an index card or sentence strip with a marker or crayon so that the word is bold. The teacher writes the word next to the child so that the child can see it written at the child's level.

Step three. The child traces the letters of the word on the index card with his index finger and says each letter as he traces it.

Step four. The child writes the word from memory without hesitation. If the child cannot do this, he continues practicing step three.

Step five. After the child writes the word from memory, he is asked to "do something" with the word such as share it with a friend, draw a picture of it, write it on the computer or chalk board, etc.

Step six. Once a week, each child reviews his words for the week with the teacher.

Words can be stored in individual index card boxes for each child or on shower curtain rings.

While this approach helps children focus on words and letters, it does not involve reading stories or informational books. For this reason, this approach should not be used as the *only* approach to beginning literacy.

Adapted from Veatch, Sawicki, Elliot, Barnett, & Blakey, 1973

➤Labeling the Room.

Another way to help children recognize letters and words is to label each item in the room (chair, table, chalk board, wall, etc.). Review these labels frequently. Eventually remove the labels and have the children read them and place them on the appropriate object in the correct place. Again, this method should be only one piece of the larger literacy puzzle for beginning readers and writers.

➤Daily News.

The Daily News is another way to help beginning and struggling readers. There are usually four basic elements of the Daily News. These include 1) the day, 2) the date, 3) the weather report, and 4) relevant news for the day. An example is shown below in figure 3.1.

Today is Tuesday, May 6, 2004. It is rainy and warm outside. We will have a fire fighter visit our class this afternoon.

Figure 3.1   Daily News

Numerous skills can be taught using Daily News. These include letters, sounds, parts of speech (nouns, verbs), compound words, possessives, etc.

➤The Beginning of the Writing Process.

Children should be given many opportunities to draw and write. Sometimes the beginning of the writing process is called "Draw and Write". Listed below are steps to use in helping students begin to draw and write:

1. Give each student a sheet of paper that is divided into the sections shown in figure 3.2. The top section is for drawing. The bottom section is for writing. Students are taught from the beginning that drawing and writing are different. The vertical line at the left side of the page is used so that students will not draw or write to the left of that margin. The reason for this is that if the child's page is eventually placed in an individual or classroom book, then the child's drawing or writing will not be covered up by the book binding.

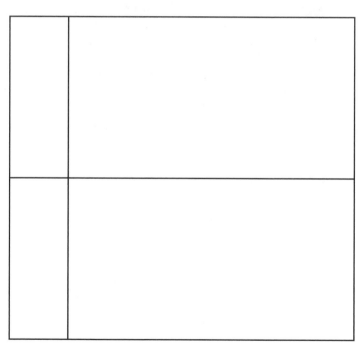

Figure 3.2   **Draw and Write activity form**

2. Ask the child to draw something on the top.
3. Ask the child to write about it on the bottom.
4. Extend the child's drawing and writing, and make note of the developmental stages of art and developmental stages of writing/spelling so that instruction can be provided that helps the child move to the next developmental level.

In **step 4** above we indicated that the teacher should make note of the developmental stages of art and the developmental stages of writing/spelling for instructional purposes. Listed in Figure 3.3 are the developmental stages of art, and the developmental stages of writing/spelling are presented in Figure 3.4

Developmental Stages of Art

1. *Random Scribbling* – The student has little control over the implement used. Child may scribble outside the paper.

2. *Controlled Scribbling* – The student has more control over the implement. Child may make more lines or loops, but the drawing is still unrecognizable to adults.

3. *Named Scribbling* – Lines become symbols. The student can tell you what she has drawn. However, what the child describes she has drawn my change, and the adult usually does not recognize what is drawn.

4. *Early Representation* – The child can recognize what she has drawn and this is "permanent," meaning the child will not change ideas about what she has drawn. An adult may recognize parts of the picture.

5. *Preschematic Drawing* – The drawing is recognizable to the adult, and the objects are appropriate size for what is portrayed.

Developmental Stages of Art adapted from Brittain (1979)

Figure 3.3   Developmental Stages of Art

Developmental Stages of Writing/Spelling

1. *Scribbling* - The child does not use letters. The child may use circles and other shapes, but conventional letters do not yet appear in her writing/spelling.

2. *Deviant spelling or letter string* – The child writes random letters that she can remember. [sTgF might stand for "hamster".]

3. *Prephonetic stage* – The child writes one, two, or three letter spellings for a word that includes some of the main consonant sounds in the word. [hrs might stand for "hamster".]

4. *Phonetic stage* – There is almost a perfect match between what the child hears and what she writes. [hamstr might stand for "hamster."]

5. *Transitional stage* – The transitional stage is different from the phonetic stage in two important ways. First, there is a vowel in every syllable, and secondly, the child spells some words correctly. [hamstir might stand for "hamster".]

6. *Correct stage* – The correct spelling stage is where formal spelling instruction should begin. This occurs usually around second grade although many programs today incorporate formal spelling lessons in first grade when children are not yet ready.

Developmental Stages of Art adapted from Gentry (1981)

Figure 3.4   Developmental Stages of Writing/Spelling

►**Shared Reading Experiences.**

According to Fisher and Medvic (2000), "shared reading is a time when the entire class gathers together to share a variety of literacy experiences by reading and discussing a variety of texts. Many of the texts are enlarged so that all the children can see the print and pictures and thus talk more easily about them" (p. 3). Share reading originated in New Zealand. Don Holdaway (1979) found that shared reading is very similar to the sharing that occurs between a parent and child during bedtime reading. Similarly, in shared reading, the teacher may read a *Big Book* to the entire class. The pictures and text are enlarged so that everyone in the room can see and participate in the activity.

While a variety of literature can be used during shared reading, predictable books are often used. Predictable books may be repetitive such as *Down by the Bay*, (Drescher, 1994) cumulative as in *There Was an Old Lady Who Swallowed a Fly*, (Taback, 1997) or a familiar sequence such as an alphabet or number sequence book.

When a Big Book is used for shared reading, there are several ways the book can be presented and used again and again. Listed below are just a few examples. Not all of the steps have to be used with every book. These are just suggestions.

1. Read the book aloud first.
2. Read the book while pointing to each word.
3. Have the children join in while you read the book.
4. Have the children dramatize the story or parts of the story.

5. At the next reading, read all but the last word on each page and have the children supply the word. This helps teach the concept of what a "word" is.

6. At the next reading, arbitrarily leave out certain words and have the students tell you the words.

7. Write the story on an overhead, blackboard, or handout so that the children can read it from a "different source."

8. Point out the concept of *letters, words,* and *phrases* as you reread the text with the children. (For example, what is the third letter on this page? What is the fourth word on this page? Etc.)

9. Tape record the story for use at the listening center.

10. Have small groups of children take one page from the book and do their own illustration and writing of that page.

11. Rewrite the story with the children using the same language pattern. (For example, students can help rewrite the book *Brown Bear, Brown Bear* (Martin, 1983) by using the children's names instead of animals. *"Carly, Carly what do you see? I see Eli looking at me. Eli, Eli, what do you see? I see Rusty looking at me, etc.)"*

Adapted from Fisher and Medvic (2000)

➤**Reading Recovery Strategies.**

Reading Recovery "has its roots in Marie Clay's own studies of young children's reading and writing behavior" (Lyons, Pinnell, & DeFord, 1993, p. 3). It is an early intervention program specifically for first grade children who are determined to be in the lowest 20% of their class. "The program includes daily, one-on-one lessons for each child. These lessons continue until the child has developed the kinds of strategies that good readers use. The lessons last 30 minutes per day and are intensive. During every minute, children are actively reading or writing; the teacher works alongside and is specially trained to bring to children's attention what they are doing that is effective" (Lyons, Pinnell, & De-Ford, 1993, pp. 4-5).

While Reading Recovery teachers are specially trained and work one-on-one with students in the program, some of the strategies used in Reading Recovery are simply good strategies that teachers of literacy in inclusive setting could use. These include the following:

1. *Reading familiar books.* Each reader has a box of familiar books and begins each lesson by re-reading a favorite book.
2. *Writing.* The child generates the writing portion of the lesson. The child can write about an experience within the book she has just read. The teacher takes notes on how to instruct the child after the child writes.
3. *First reading of a new book.* The teacher introduces a new book for the child to read. The teacher helps the child use strategies to determine unknown words and comprehend the text.
4. *Skills practice.* Based on the child's reading and writing, the teacher and child work on the skills for which the child is ready.

Adapted from Lyons, Pinnell, and DeFord (1993)

►Teaching the Alphabet in Context.

In every approach mentioned in this chapter, there are opportunities to teach the alphabet in context. Using environmental print, the teacher can point out the letters of familiar logos. Using the Key Vocabulary Approach, the teacher can help the child identify every letter in the word she has chosen. When the teacher has labeled the familiar objects around the room, lessons can be taught on the letters as well as the words found around the classroom. In Daily News, finding specific letters can be one of the tasks of the day. Similarly, in the beginnings of the writing process, shared reading experiences, and Reading Recovery strategies teaching the alphabet in context is part of each approach. Teaching the alphabet in the context of authentic reading and writing is more appropriate than using a "letter of the week" approach (Kirkland, Aldridge, & Kuby, 2002).

In this chapter we have described how readiness is defined and considered eight important ways to begin teaching reading and writing at the very beginning stage of literacy. These methods or strategies can also be used with older, struggling readers who are still in the beginning stages of literacy.

While there are four cueing systems mentioned in chapter one, it is important to note that the *No Child Left Behind Act* is now in place, and a skills-based approach to reading is being advocated by the federal government. Some states and administrators are interpreting this to mean that a strong phonics based program should be used. While this is not necessarily the view of the authors of this book, we have included a description of what constitutes an explicit, direct, and systematic phonics program in the next chapter.

REFERENCES

Aldridge, J., Kirkland, L., & Kuby, P. (2002) *Jumpstarters: Integrating environmental Print throughout the curriculum* (3rd ed.). Birmingham, AL: Campus Press.

Aldridge, J., & Rust, D. (1987) A beginning reading strategy. *Academic Therapy,* 22(3), 323-236.

Brittain, W.L. (1979) *Creativity, art, and the young child.* New York: Macmillan.

Drescher, H. (1994) *Down by the bay: A traditional song.* Tuscon, AZ: Good Year Books.

Fisher, B., & Medvic, E. (2000). *Perspectives on shared reading: Planning and practice.* Portsmouth, NH: Heinemann.

Gentry, R.J. (1981). Learning to read developmentally. *Reading Teacher,* 34, 378-381).

Holdaway, D. (1979). *Foundations of literacy.* Portsmouth, NH: Heinemann.

Kirkland, L., Aldridge, J., & Kuby, P. (1991). Environmental print and the kindergarten classroom. *Reading Improvement,* 28, 219 – 222.

Lyons, C.A., Pinnell, G.S., & Deford, D.E. (1993). *Partners in learning: Teachers and children in Reading Recovery.* New York: Teachers College Press.

Martin, B. (1983) *Brown bear, brown bear, what do you see?* New York: Henry Holt & Company.

Mophett, M., & Washurne, C. (1931). When should children begin to read? *Elementary School Journal,* March Issue.

Taback, S. (1997) *There was an old lady who swallowed a fly.* New York: Viking Juvenile.

U.S. Department of Education, Office of Elementary and Secondary Education, *No Child Left Behind: A Desktop Reference,* Washington, DC, 2002.

Veatch, J., Sawicki, F., Elliot, G., Barnett, E., & Blakey, J. (1973). *Key words to reading: The language experience approach begins.* Columbus, OH: Charles E. Merrill.

CHAPTER FOUR

Current Assessment Practices

Much emphasis has been placed on assessment in recent years due to the accountability demanded by the No Child Left Behind (NCLB) act of 2001. NCLB requires that students be tested each year and that schools show that students are making adequate yearly progress (Aldridge & Goldman, 2007). Through the pressure of this standardized testing, teachers must remember the purpose of assessment. According to the National Forum on Assessment (1995), the primary goal of assessment should be to improve student learning. The scores of each student may be entered into a database in order to make judgments about the success or failure of the school, and this pressure does trickle down to the classroom teachers, but teachers should not lose sight of the reason for assessment. Teachers must look beyond the political rhetoric and see the students in their charge. Teachers must use the tools that they are given to ensure that student learning is improved. The purpose of this chapter is to discuss a widely used standardized test currently being used in primary classrooms to meet the requirements of NCLB and to examine ways that teachers can take the information gleaned from this test to help their students learn. Alternative means of assessment that may be beneficial if used in conjunction with standardized testing will also be discussed.

Dynamic Indicators of Basic Early Literacy Skills (DIBELS)

The Dynamic Indicators of Basic Early Literacy Skills (DIBELS) test has become so prevalent that in many schools "DIBEL" has become a verb referring to the testing of children: "Have you DIBELed all of your students?" According to the official DIBELS website, in the 2004-2005 school year, the DIBELS test was used in 8,293 schools across 49 states. Many states have mandated that this test be given in kindergarten through third grade as a measure of adequate yearly progress to meet the accountability demanded by NCLB. If teachers are to truly use this assessment to improve student learning, then they must understand what the test is, what information it supplies, and the strengths and limitations of this information.

The DIBELS test was designed to test three of the "Big Ideas" in early literacy. The areas addressed by DIBELS are phonological awareness, alphabetic principle, and fluency with connected text (Institute for the Development of Educational Achievement, 2002).

►Phonological Awareness.

Phonological awareness "refers to an individual's awareness of the sound structure, or phonological structure, of spoken word" (Gillon, 2004, p. 2). This means that it is the awareness that words are made up of sounds. It does not refer to *written word*. At the level of phonological awareness, the child is not expected to make sound-letter correspondences. She is only expected to hear the sounds that make up individual words. There are two aspects of the DIBELS test that measure phonological awareness. These are the "Initial Sound Fluency" (ISF) test and the "Phoneme Segmentation Fluency" (PSF) test (Institute for the Development of Educational Achievement, 2002).

The Initial Sound Fluency test is given to pre-school and kindergarten children in order to assess their phonological awareness. According to the official DIEBLS website:

> The examiner presents four pictures to the child, names each picture, and then asks the child to identify (i.e., point to or say) the picture that begins with the sound produced orally by the examiner. For example, the examiner says, "This is sink, cat, gloves, and hat. Which picture begins with /s/?" and the student points to the correct picture. The child is also asked to orally produce the beginning sound for an orally presented word that matches one of the given pictures. The examiner calculates the amount of time taken to identify/produce the correct sound and converts the score into the number of initial sounds correct in a minute.

The other DIBELS task designed to assess a child's phonemic awareness is the Phoneme Segmentation Fluency (PSF) test. The DIBELS website reports the following about the PSF test:

> The PSF task is administered by the examiner orally presenting words of three to four phonemes. It requires the student to produce verbally the individual phonemes for each word. For example, the examiner says "sat," and the student

says "/s/ /a/ /t/" to receive three possible points for the word. After the student responds, the examiner presents the next word, and the number of correct phonemes produced in one minute determines the final score.

➤Alphabetic Principle.

The alphabetic principle refers to "the fact that the sounds in oral language *(phonemes)* can be represented by written letters *(graphemes)*" (Rathvon, 2004, p. 66). This is the level at which a child makes letter-sound correspondence. It involves both the spoken and the written word. To assess a child's knowledge about the alphabetic principle, the DIBELS test uses a task called "Nonsense Word Fluency" (NWF). This test, according to the DIBELS website, "assesses a child's knowledge of letter-sound correspondences as well their ability to blend letters together to form unfamiliar 'nonsense' (e.g., fik, lig, etc.) words". The website goes on to describe the administration of the NWF test:

> The student is presented an 8.5" x 11" sheet of paper with randomly ordered VC and CVC nonsense words (e.g., sig, rav, ov) and asked to produce verbally the individual letter sound of each letter or verbally produce, or read, the whole nonsense word. For example, if the stimulus word is "vaj" the student could say /v/ /a/ /j/ or say the word /vaj/ to obtain a total of three letter-sounds correct. The student is allowed 1 minute to produce as many letter-sounds as he/she can, and the final score is the number of letter-sounds produced correctly in one minute.

►Fluency with Connected Text.

There is much debate over just what "fluency" means (Rathvon, 2004). Myers and Felton (1999) describe reading fluency as "the ability to read connected text rapidly, smoothly, effortlessly, and automatically with little conscious attention to the mechanics of reading" (p. 284). The DIBELS task used to measure a student's ability to read connected text is called the "Oral Reading Fluency" (ORF) test. According to the website of the Institute for the Development of Educational Achievement (2002), The DIBELS ORF test is:

> a standardized set of passages and administration procedures   designed to (a) identify children who may need additional instructional support, and (b) monitor progress toward instructional goals. The passages are calibrated for the goal level of reading for each grade level. Student performance is measured by having students read a passage aloud for one minute. Words omitted, substituted, and hesitations of more than three seconds are scored as errors. Words self-corrected within three seconds are scored as accurate. The number of correct words per minute from the passage is the oral reading fluency rate.

Using the Information

After the administration of these tests for phonological awareness, awareness of the alphabetic principle, and fluency of connected text, the teacher is left with number scores. The ISF and PSF tests give number scores for the number of initial sounds a child can produce in one minute and the number of phonemes the child can segment in one minute, respectively. The NWF test gives the number of letter sounds a child can identify in one minute from a list of nonsense words. The ORF test gives the number of words per minute that a child can read from grade-level appropriate text. With these four numbers in hand, what is the teacher supposed to be able to do?

For the primary teacher, DIBELS offers scores that measure a child's phonological awareness, knowledge of the alphabetic principle, and oral reading fluency (at grade one and beyond.) In order to avoid placing too much emphasis on the students' scores on this ONE measure of their literacy development, teachers need to focus instead on authentic activities that will enhance children's development in these three areas. Below are ideas to help develop children's phonological awareness, knowledge of the alphabetic principle, and oral reading fluency.

As discussed earlier, phonological awareness deals with the spoken word. To develop children's ability to discern the sounds of spoken language, the most important thing teachers can do is to develop children's oral language. In other words, there needs to be lots of words! Many children who are labeled as being "at-risk" for failure in reading actually have a deficit in their oral language development (Gentile, 2004). To combat problems that stem from low oral language development, children need to be engaged in conversation. It is not enough to *talk to* children. If this was the case, oral language development would be optimized by sitting children in front of the television! Children need to be *active participants* in rich conversations. Studies show that the *quantity* of conversation is not nearly as important as the *quality* of the conversations to which children are exposed (August, Carlo, Dressler, & Snow, 2005). Children need to hear sentences of differing lengths and structures, and they need to be encouraged to use sentences that vary in complexity.

A teacher can assess a child's oral language development by listening to the child. Listen to the child in casual conversation, and note the complexity of the sentences the child uses. Is every sentence a simple subject/verb sentence? Does the child use prepositional phrases? Does the child link sentences with conjunctions or with adverbial clauses? Gentile (2004) reports that children progress through these types of sentences in a predictable order, and the kinds of sentences a child has at his command give valuable insight into his oral language development.

With this information in hand, a teacher can enhance the child's oral language development, and thus promote phonological awareness, by encouraging the child to use sentences that just exceed the child's current ability. Consider the following exchange:

Teacher: Do you have a pet?
Child: a dog.
Teacher: You have a dog? What color is your dog?
Child: It's brown and gots white spots.
Teacher: You have a brown dog with white spots. What its name?
Child: Rags.
Teacher: You have a brown dog with white spots, and his name is Rags. Can you say that?
Child: I have a brown dog with white spots, and his name is Rags.

This is a very simple exchange, but it demonstrates that a teacher can coax a child into giving enough information to form a sentence that is clearly more complex than the child uses himself. When the teacher forms the sentence and has the child repeat the sentence, the child is encouraged to use more complex oral language. This works well in casual one-on-one conversation. To extend this activity to a group setting, the teacher can have children work to retell a story or describe a recent shared experience. Each child can give a sentence, and the story grows with each addition. The teacher returns to the beginning several times in the telling of the story in order to give the children the opportunity to repeat their parts. The teacher can help children to elaborate on vocabulary and sentence structure as the story grows. Once the story is completed, and the children have repeated it several times, the teacher can extend the difficulty of the activity by having the children exchange their "parts". The children mix their order but try to keep the story the same. This gives students the chance to practice reproducing the sentences that they have heard repeated.

Knowledge of sound-letter correspondence is enhanced through authentic opportunities to use written language. It is through writing that children show their proficiency with the alphabetic principle (Kamii & Manning, 2005). The teacher must do two things to use written language as a tool to develop and assess the alphabetic principle. Students must be given the opportunity to write. They must be encouraged to use their own spellings to express themselves through writing. This happens best in natural settings and with authentic reasons for writing. The teacher can help this along by making writing materials available in all areas of the room. If the room is arranged in centers, each center should have paper and writing implements. The teacher can model reasons for real writing. For example, if Chase has made a great block structure, the teacher might say, "This is wonderful! I'd like to remember how we did this. I think I'll write it down." When children see the teacher using writing to communicate, they will also begin to use writing to express themselves. Once the children are writing, the teacher must then assess the finished products for evidence of phonological awareness and the alphabetic principle. Kamii and Manning (2005) show different stages of writing development, but the thing to remember is that if you can read a child's "invented spellings", then the child is phonemically aware (Kamii & Manning, 2005).

For teachers who are not yet comfortable with informal teacher observation as a means of assessment, there are more formal ways to evaluate children's development in phonological awareness, alphabetic principle, and reading fluency. Lance Gentile (2004) provides teachers with a user-friendly informal assessment which uses repeated sentences, drawing, and retelling of a story to assess children's oral language development. The *Oral Language Acquisition Inventory* (Gentile, 2004) also includes activities to use once the child's developmental level has been established.

To assess children's early literacy development, Marie Clay (2002) offers several easy to use assessments. Teachers can assess children's ability to name letters as well as their sound-letter correspondence with the tasks explained in *An Observation Survey of Early Literacy Achievement* (Clay, 2002). Teachers are offered sound theoretical advice about observing children's early literacy development and are given the tools to help children to develop their abilities. Clay also gives instruction about how to keep running records of children's reading of connected text.

Once children are reading text, teachers can use the *Qualitative Reading Inventory* (QRI) (Leslie & Caldwell, 2001) to assess students' abilities. Using this informal assessment, the teacher can observe students' reading behavior and can determine strengths and weaknesses. The assessment offers grade level narrative and expository text for grade levels from pre-primer through upper middle school. Several texts at each grade level ensure that the teacher can use the QRI repeatedly with students. The QRI allows teachers to assess reading fluency without the pressure of a stop-watch. Students who are intimidated by the pressure to perform may do better with this assessment.

Standardized tests, such as DIBELS, that are used to meet the requirements of NCLB give indicators of very specific skills that are a part of reading. Teachers can use this information to identify children who may need extra help. Rather than focusing on the test scores, teachers should offer authentic activities that allow children to use spoken and written language. There are many informal assessments that can give more information about a child's abilities. Educators need to be careful not to rely too heavily on any one measure of a child's literacy development. To do so may ignore the strengths of some students.

REFERENCES

Aldridge, J., & Goldman, R. (2007) *Current Issues in Education* (2nd Ed.). Boston: Allyn & Bacon.

August, D., Carlo, M., Dressler, C., & Snow, C. (2005) The critical role of vocabulary development for English language learners. *Learning Disabilities Research and Practice,* (20)1, 50-57.

Gentile, L.M. (2004) *Oral language acquisition inventory (OLAI): Linking research and theory to assessment and instruction.* New Market, Ontario: Dominie Press.

Gillon, G.T. (2004). *Phonological awareness: From research to practice.* New York: Guilford Press.

Institute for the Development of Educational Achievement. (2002) *What are the Dynamic Indicators of Basic Early Literacy Skills or DIBELS ?* http://reading.uoregon.edu/assessment/dibels_ what.php. Accessed January 23, 2007.

Kamii, C. & Manning, M. (2005) Dynamic indicators of basic early literacy skills (DIBELS): A tool for evaluating student learning? *Journal of Research in Childhood Education.* 20(2), 75-90.

Meyer, M.S., & Felton, R.H. (1999) Repeated reading to enhance fluency: Old approaches and new directions. *Annals of Dyslexia,* 49, 283-306.

National Forum on Assessment. (1995), *Principals and indicators for student assessment systems.* Cambridge, MA: National Center for Fair and Open Testing.

Rathvon, N. (2004) *Early reading assessment: A practitioner's handbook.* New York: Guilford Press.

CHAPTER FIVE

The Importance of Oral Language Development

In Chapter Two we described oral language development as the foundation or fuel for learning to read and write. We also mentioned that some struggling readers have had limited experience with oral language development (Barton, 2004). When children reach the early elementary grades, the focus of reading in many schools moves away from oral language to the "big five" goals of Reading First. These are phonemic awareness, phonics, vocabulary, fluency, and comprehension. While social interaction and oral language can be embedded in these five, they usually are not. A lot of instruction is provided concerning learning to read and write while any emphasis of oral language development is severely diminished. This is especially true in traditional, transmission oriented classrooms in which students are expected to sit in their seats quietly completing one worksheet after another. In fact, in such classrooms, oral language is often discouraged as the teacher reminds the students to "work quietly and do not talk to your neighbor."

This chapter is concerned with enhancing oral language development. We begin with a scenario in which interactions between young children and their parents are used to show the importance of oral language development. Then we describe six ways to encourage oral language development in the classroom.

Learning Oral Language

SCENARIO: Consider the following three parental interactions with 3-year-old children in the grocery store. In the first interaction, the mother and child move down the aisles of the food store, and the child sees and reaches for a cantaloupe. She asks, "What's that?" Her mother responds, "Stop that!" and moves on. The second guardian and child approach the cantaloupe, and this child also asks "What's that?" This time the adult answers, "That's a cantaloupe, but you wouldn't like it." In the third interaction, after the child's question of "What's that?", the adult enthusiastically explains, "Why that's called a 'cantaloupe.' Look at how round it is. Let's smell it. Oh, what does it smell like to you? Does it look like the honey dew melon we had for lunch? Let's take it home and try it. What do you think it will taste like?"

All three of these adult-child interactions are common in the grocery store. While the second adult's response was better than that of the first, in the third interaction the parent engages the child in language with questions, wonder, and excitement. This is what is needed for a child to develop a rich vocabulary. As noted in Chapter Two, "three-year-old children in professional families" can have a rich vocabulary that is "as large as that of the parents...who were on welfare" (Barton, 2004, p. 10).

When children with limited interactions, such as those of the first two parents in our scenario, enter school, their language development may be so limited that learning to read and write appears to be an insurmountable task. Then, in traditional classrooms they are requested to sit quietly and not talk, do their worksheets, and spend a large percentage of their day working silently and alone. What is needed is a classroom with rich oral language experiences. Six ways to develop a room which enhances student interaction and meaningful talk include: 1) a class meeting time, 2) relevant transactional and transformational teaching, 3) reading aloud to children, 4) using environmental print, 5) incorporating meaningful "show and tell", and 6) encouraging oral representation of learning experiences.

Class Meeting Time

Many teachers hold class meetings with the intention of enhancing oral language. In early childhood this is sometimes called "circle time" or "morning meeting". The problem is that these meetings are often directed and controlled entirely by the teacher, and this does little to develop children's oral language capabilities. The discussion might include daily news, calendar time, weather report, and explanations about what activities the class will be involved with during the day. However, most of the talking is done by the teacher. Class meeting time and oral language development are enhanced if the children are more responsible for the class meeting. Good teachers use class meeting time to encourage vocabulary and oral language development. Students are encouraged to take charge of daily news, calendar time, the weather report, asking questions and giving examples during this important ritual during morning meeting. Afternoon meetings or end-of-the-day sessions are also important for students to verbally describe what they did and to ask questions they might have.

The school day is often filled with many **transmission** teaching examples. Transmission usually occurs when the teacher is talking and the students are supposed to be listening. Transmission is necessary for children to learn social knowledge. For example, the smartest child in the world will not know what the letter "a" is called unless someone tells her. Some transmission is necessary but when the entire day is spent in teacher talk and student silence, then oral language development is severely limited. What is needed is **transactional** and **transformational** interactions.

➤**Transaction** occurs when students are working in groups, talking together, and learning from one another. One of the best ways oral language develops through transaction is through the **project approach** (Katz & Chard, 2000). When students explore a chosen topic, they must discuss what they know, what they want to know more about, and how they will investigate it. Transactional learning also takes place through constructivist mathematics. When students have to share and describe how they arrived at the answer to a math problem, they must develop the oral language capacity to explain their answer to others. A transactional curriculum provides numerous, rich opportunities for language development.

➤**Transformation** is another curriculum approach that propels oral language learning. A transformational classroom is one that seeks to make a difference in the world (Aldridge & Goldman, 2007). Transformation is inquiry based. Students "inquire" or ask questions about topics they want to know more about, but, unlike transaction, the purpose of transformation is to help others. A transformational room is one in which social interactions are constantly taking place. Vocabulary is developed and oral language is valued, encouraged, and supported.

Reading Aloud to Children

Nancy Qualls, a renowned Jungian analyst, reports that her oral language was enhanced by her fifth grade teacher. After lunch every day, her teacher read Shakespeare to the class. Nancy and other students in her class asked the teacher to explain many of the words they did not understand which were read aloud by the teacher. Suffice it to say, a teacher should read to her class every day at a set time. The read aloud should be challenging and on the students' listening level.

Environmental Print

Environmental print is defined as the authentic print children see all around them every day. Billboards, stop signs, food labels, fast food packages, newspapers, and the names of stores and businesses are all examples of environmental print (Kirkland, Aldridge, & Kuby, 2007). Environmental print is another authentic way to encourage language development. Teachers can make an environmental print box in which children can bring and deposit logos and labels. During class meeting time, before read aloud time, or even during a special time devoted to environmental print, the teacher can pull out the logos and labels brought to school that day. Then, oral language development can be encouraged when the teacher asks, "Who brought the napkin from Pizza Hut? I see Meredith did. Tell us about your experience at Pizza Hut?" Meredith's oral language is then scaffolded by the teacher who extends and refines Meredith's descriptions.

"My grandma took me to Pizza Hut last night."

"Tell me more," responds the teacher.

A discussion follows that centers around Meredith's story of her trip to dinner the night before with her grandmother. Other students are encouraged to ask Meredith questions. The teacher guides the discussion with the important goal of extending and refining oral language development.

Meaningful Show and Tell

Show and tell has been a part of elementary classrooms for decades. However, show and tell usually involves a one way street. That is, the teller describes what she has brought and the class is expected to listen. There are however, other ways to improve show and tell with the goal of oral language development in mind. For example, a variation on show and tell is for the student to describe what she has brought for show and tell, without the other students seeing it. The describer has to give vivid and appropriate explanations for other students to guess what she brought.

Another variation would be to have students sit in pairs, back to back. One student describes what she brought for show and tell while the other has to guess. Then, roles are reversed and the other student describes the object he brought for show and tell. Both students have to work on speaking (describing) and listening in order to succeed at this form of show and tell. Making show and tell more authentic, meaningful, and interactive is another way to stretch children's oral language.

Oral Representation of Learning

Early on in elementary school, teachers resort to paper and pencil tests to measure student learning. With the advent of No Child Left Behind this practice has drastically increased. There are other ways students can represent what they have learned. One way that also increases oral language is for students to orally represent what they have learned. That is, students are asked to explain what they have learned to a small group of peers, the whole class, or the teacher. If teachers scaffold children's explanations, oral language representations will improve over time and benefit every child's oral language facility.

In Chapter Five we have discussed the salience of oral language development and provided several suggestions for enhancing its development in the classroom. Class meetings, transaction and transformational learning, reading aloud to children, environmental print, meaningful show and tell, and allowing students to orally represent what they have learned are all examples of ways oral language development can be enhanced. In Chapter Six we describe phonemic awareness activities for struggling readers that should improve students' understanding of the sounds or phonemes of our language.

REFERENCES

Aldridge, J., & Goldman, R. (2007). *Current issues and trends in education.* Boston: Allyn and Bacon.

Barton, P. E. (2004). Why does the gap persist? *Educational Leadership, 62*(3), 9-13.

Katz, L., & Chard, S. (2000). *Engaging children's minds: The project approach* (2nd ed.). Norwood, NJ: Ablex.

Kirkland, Aldridge, J., & Kuby, P. (2007). *Integrating environmental print across the curriculum, preK-3: Making literacy instruction meaning.* Thousand Oaks, CA: Corwin Press.

CHAPTER SIX

Phonemic Awareness

"Phonemes are the smallest sounds in spoken words" (Enz, 2006, p. 19). The important word here is "sounds". One way we can remember what phonemes are is by thinking about a phone. I hear a "sound" on the phone. Graphemes, on the other hand, are the written forms of sounds. When we "graph" something, we put it on paper. We write the sound on paper. So, phonemic awareness is concerned with sounds and not the written representations of them. Phonemic awareness is defined as "the ability to notice, think about, and work with the individual sounds in spoken words. Before children learn to read print, they need to become aware of how the sounds in words work. They must understand that words are made up of speech sounds, or phonemes" (Center for the Improvement of Early Reading Achievement, 2001, p. 2).

If phonemic awareness activities are not meaningful, relevant, and fun for struggling readers, they may need additional support. This short chapter provides three simple ways to enhance phonemic awareness through 1) children's names, 2) music, and 3) storytelling.

Children's Names

Children are usually fascinated by their own names and the names of the other children in the class. Using the children's names is a great way to improve phonemic awareness. Here are a few examples of how children's names can be used.

The teacher says, "Today we are going to listen to the sounds in our names. I hear the /m/ sound in Maria. Who else has a name that begins with the /m/ sound like Maria's name?" Children raise their hands and a lively discussion develops about the sounds or phonemes we hear at the beginning of the names of all the children in the class. Over time, after listening and identifying beginning sounds, names can be used to discuss ending sounds.

The instructor can say, "I hear the /m/ sound at the end of Tom's name. Do we have anyone else in our class whose name ends with the /m/ sound?" This process can also be used to identify medial or middle sounds in children's names.

Music

Listening to and singing songs is another way phonemic awareness can be developed. For example, in the song, "My Bonnie Lies Over the Ocean, " children can be asked to stand up every time they ear the /b/ sound and then to sit down the next time they hear the /b/ sound in the song.

In the song, "This Old Man" students can be asked to supply the rhyming word for some of the verses. For example, "This old man, he played two, he played nicknack on my_____." Extensions of this can also encourage phonemic awareness through rhymes. "Can you think of any other words that rhyme with 'two' and 'shoe'?"

There are plenty of songs that have rhyming words. Other examples include, "The Ants go Marching One by One," (Bernal, 1993) "Jump Jim Joe," (Amidon & Amidon, 1991) and "My Aunt Came Back" (Cummings, 1998). Many struggling readers have difficulty with phonemic awareness. Using songs provides added support for its development.

Storytelling

Storytelling and inventions provide another support for phonemic awareness development. Numerous stories can be invented by thinking about sounds. For example, "Class, we're going on a fishing trip, and we're going to take things with us that begin with the /m/ sound. What are some things we can take with us that start with the /m/ sound?"

Children's names, music, and storytelling are all appropriate ways to enhance phonemic awareness. Many phonemic awareness activities spill over into phonics. Phonics instruction is concerned with "the relationships between the letters (graphemes) of written language and the individual sounds (phonemes) of spoken language" (Center for the Improvement of Early Reading Achievement, 2001, p. 12). Chapter Seven is concerned with teaching phonics and provides a suggested sequence for teaching phonics.

REFERENCES

Amidon, M.A., & Amidon, P. (1991). *Jump jim joe: Great singing games for children.* Battleboro, VT: New England Dancing Masters Productions.

Bernal, R. (1993). *The ants go marching one by one.* New York: Scholastic, Inc.

Center for the Improvement of Early Reading Achievement (2001). *Putting reading first: The research building blocks for teaching children to read.* Bethesda, MD: National Institute of Child Health and Human Development.

Cummings, P. (1998). *My aunt came back.* New York: Harper Festival.

Enz, B. (2006). Phonemic awareness: Activities that make sounds come alive. In C. Cummins (Ed.), *Understanding and implementing Reading First initiatives: The changing role of administrators* (pp. 18-3). Neward, DE: International Reading Association.

CHAPTER SEVEN

Teaching Phonics

Just what is phonics? Phonics "refers to instructional practices that emphasize how spellings are related to speech sounds in systematic ways" (National Research Council, 1998, p. 52). In more practical terms, phonics is "instruction in how the sounds of speech are represented by letters and spellings" (National Research Council, 1998, p. 55).

Over the years there have been hundreds of phonics instruction programs. Some phonics programs have been *synthetic* which means the focus on these programs is on the learner sounding out the individual or isolated phonemes that make up a word. For example, in the word "Cat" the learner would be asked to sound out /k/ then /a/ and then/t/. There are numerous problems with this – one of the most important of which is the fact that an isolated sound does not translate into the exact phoneme in the word. For instance, if you ask a child to sound out each phoneme in the word "bag" the result would be "buh" "a" "guh".

Some phonics programs have been *analytic* which means the learner is asked to consider the entire word and then "analyze" the sounds. In an analytic approach the word "cat" would be considered as a whole, but the learner might be asked to think of other words that begin with the letter "c" or words that end in the letter "t".

We recommend that phonics be considered as only one piece of the reading puzzle. Remember, in Chapter One we describe four cueing systems. These were the *graphophonic, syntactic, semantic,* and *pragmatic* cueing systems, *all* of which are necessary for literacy. However, the purpose of this chapter is to describe what is known as the explicit, direct, and systematic teaching of phonics. The *No Child Left Behind Act* of 2001 is now a reality, and the federal government is funding only scientifically based reading programs. Many of the approved reading programs are based on the explicit teaching of phonics.

There is no one way to teach phonics explicitly, directly, or systematically. However, most phonics programs that are designed to teach phonics explicitly are written using a *scope* and *sequence. Scope* refers to the range of skills that are to be taught. In other words, what are all of the sounds that will be taught? *Sequence* is the order in which the phonemes or skills are to be taught. Remembering that there are hundreds of phonics programs, *most* phonics programs include the following skills listed below. An example of an explicit scope and sequence that is representative of many phonics programs is presented here. Teachers are expected to teach the following skills in the order and in this way.

An Example of A Scope and Sequence Chart for Teaching Phonics

The students will be able to:

1. Associate words using the beginning consonant sounds. (cat, hat)
2. Associate words using the ending consonant sounds. (cat, cap)
3. Associate words with consonants found in the medial position. (letter, beggar)
4. Use the "beginning, ending, and middle" strategy when spelling/writing. (What sound do you hear at the beginning of the word? Ending of the word? Middle of the word?)
5. Know and use consonant digraphs (sh, wh, th, TH, ch, ph, and gh). (shoe, think, this, chop, phone, and cough)
6. Name the ending sound of "ed". (wanted, moved, and liked)
7. Know and use short vowel sounds. (Key words used: apple, egg, igloo, octopus, and umbrella)
8. Recognize word families and make rhyming words by adding beginning consonant sounds. For example, for the word family "all", the student could make words such as ball, call, and fall.
9. Know and use the following consonant blends (br, cr, dr, fr, gr, pr, sk, sm, sn, st, sw, bl, cl, fl, gl, pl, and sl); (bring, cry, dress, free, grass, pretty, skim, small, sneeze, start, sweet, blue, flip, glue, play, sleep)
10. Know and use the following 3 letter consonant blends (str, spr, spl, scr, sch, thr, chr); (street,

spring, splash, scream, school, throw, chronicle)

11. Recognize more word families and use them to make words. For example, for "ow" the student could make words such as know, flow, and snow. For "ow" the student could make words such as now, cow, and how.

12. Know and use long vowel sounds. (Key words used: ape, eel, ice, oats, ukelele)

13. Know the following sounds of y: yellow, play, pretty, my, myth, cycle, toy.

14. Know and use the hard and soft sounds of c (hard: cat, cot, cut – soft: cent, city, cycle)

15. Know and use the hard and soft sounds of g (hard: gas, got, gum – soft: giraffe, gentle, gypsy)

16. Know and use words with the consonant-vowel-consonant (cvc) pattern (bat, net, pit, cot, nut)

17. Know and use words with the consonant-vowel-consonant-final e (cvce) pattern (date, Pete, kite, note, tune)

18. Know and use words with the consonant-vowel-vowel-consonant (cvvc) pattern (rain, bean, boat, suit)

19. Know and use "r" controlled vowels (car, her, first, for, fur)

20. Know and use accented syllable rules.

21. Know how and when to add plurals to words.

22. Know how to add "ing" to cvc and cvce pattern words (hop = hopping; hope = hoping)

23. Know when to change the "y" to "i" before adding "es" (plurals).

24. Know silent letters in kn, wr, gn, ps, pn. (know, wrong, gnaw, psychology, pheumonia)
25. Know when to drop the "f" and add "ves" to make the plural. (knife/knives)
26. Know the similarity in the sounds of "x" and "ks" in "box" and "blocks".
27. Generalize syllabication rules as in "pu-pil" and "lit-tle".
28. Hyphenate words using syllabication rules.
29. Know the meaning of affixes (prefixes and suffixes) and use them appropriately.
30. Know the schwa sound (which is the short u sound in an unaccented syllable).
31. Know vowel digraphs (au, aw, ew, short oo, long oo, ou, ow). (faught, saw, few, foot, noon, through, and show)
32. Know diphthongs such as "oi, oy,ou, and ow". (boil, boy, ouch, and cow)
33. Determine what sound the "o" makes in exceptions to the rule such as "woman" and "women".
34. Know, can identify, and give exaples of the following terms: heteronym, homograph, homonym, and homophone.
35. Know when "a" makes the short "o" sound. (water, watch)
36. Know when "or" makes the "ur" sound. (work, worm, word)
37. Know when "ar" makes the "or" sound. (war, warm, wart)
38. Know the following sounds of "s": s, z, sh, zh. (sit, shoes, sugar, measure)
39. Know the following sounds of "x": ks, gz, z. (excuse, exit, xylophone)

40. Know the following sounds of "z": z, s, zh (zoo, waltz, azure)
41. Know the following sounds of "ch": ch, k, sh, kw (chew, chorus, chateau, choir)
42. Know the sounds of tion and sion which include shun (for tion) and zhun and shun (for sion).
43. Know and can identify open syllables (those ending in a vowel sound).
44. Know and can identify closed syllables (those ending in a consonant sound).

Summary

While there is no one way to teach phonics, we have presented an example of a scope and sequence chart that provides a teacher with a general guide for teaching a specific set of skills in a particular sequence. Phonics is just one part of the reading program. There are other cueing systems including semantic, syntactic, and pragmatic systems that must also be taught to give students all of the tools necessary to determine and understand unknown words.

REFERENCE

National Reading Council (1998). *Preventing reading difficulties in young children.* Washington, DC: National Academy Press.

U.S. Department of Education, office of Elementary and Secondary Education, *No Child Left Behind: A Desktop Reference.* Washington, DC, 2002.

CHAPTER EIGHT

Vocabulary

According to the Center for the Improvement of Early Reading Achievement (2001), "Children learn the meanings of most words indirectly, through everyday experiences with oral and written language" (p. 35). However, some vocabulary must be taught. According to Flood, Lapp, and Flood (2006) teachers most commonly ask four important questions when thinking about teaching vocabulary. These include:

> "1. How many words can I teach in one year? In one lesson?
> 2. What words should I teach?
> 3. How may encounters or exposures are necessary before a student 'owns' a new vocabulary word?
> 4. How can I effectively teach vocabulary?"
> (p. 46).

Typically, children learn about 400 new words per year, but how many words can be taught in one lesson? According to Flood, Lapp, and Flood (2006), more than five new words in one lesson can tax a student's memory.

The answer to the question, "What words should I teach?" can be overwhelming because the possibilities are endless. However, an appropriate plan for supporting struggling readers' vocabulary development is to teach words that will be used often and to teach content area words. It usually takes around 8 to 10 encounters with a word before students own it. For struggling readers, this number of exposures may need to be greater (Flood, Lapp, & Flood, 2006).

How should vocabulary be taught to struggling readers? Vocabulary is inextricably tied to comprehension. Chapter Ten is a lengthy chapter that considers multiple ways to enhance comprehension. Most of the strategies found in Chapter Ten are also important for vocabulary development. Examples include K-W-L, K-N-L, pyramiding, webbing, and Venn diagrams. See Chapter Ten for these important strategies for teaching vocabulary as well as comprehension.

REFERENCES

Center for the Improvement of Early Reading Achievement (2001). *Putting reading first: The research building blocks for teaching children to read.* Bethesda, MD: National Institute of Child Health and Human Development.

Flood, J., Lapp, D., & Flood, S. (2006). Vocabulary instruction: New ideas and time-tested strategies. In C. Cummins (ED.), *Understanding and implementing Reading First initiatives: The changing role of administrators* (pp. 42-59). Newark, DE: International Reading Association.

CHAPTER NINE

Fluency

Fluency is defined as "the ability to read a text accurately and quickly. When fluent readers read silently, they recognize words automatically" (Center for the Improvement of Early Reading Achievement, 2001, p. 22). Teaching fluency to struggling readers presents a real dilemma for teachers. Although there are other tests that measure fluency (see Rasinski, 2004), the assessment that is most often used to measure fluency is the Dynamic Indicators of Basic Early Literacy Skills or DIBELS (Institute for the Development of Educational Achievement, 2002). By the end of second grade, students are expected to see and say 90 nonsense words in 60 seconds. However, many educators believe that fluency should be tied to comprehension. When individuals read, they adjust their fluency depending on the difficulty and nature of the text. So, what's a teacher to do?

A compromise for "teaching fluency" is to try and balance assessment procedures with what we know about fluency and the need for adjusting in order to comprehend a text. To help struggling readers, one answer is to play a game called **Category Fluency**. Students are asked to read words by categories that are relevant to them or curriculum related as fast as they can. Listed below are 10 examples of categories that can be used for this game. While we would never recommend using a stop watch or timing fluency, the reality is, most students will be time tested on fluency. For this reason, students can time themselves on reading words by the following categories if you (or they) desire.

- ➤ sports words
- ➤ car (or vehicle) words
- ➤ animal words
- ➤ plant words
- ➤ curriculum words
- ➤ television words
- ➤ scary words
- ➤ the names of students in our class words
- ➤ community words
- ➤ job or career words

As we have mentioned, fluency should be tied to comprehension. Chapter Ten provides numerous strategies for teaching comprehension as well as ways to teach struggling readers to monitor their own comprehension.

REFERENCES

Center for the Improvement of Early Reading Achievement (2001). *Putting reading first: The research building blocks for teaching children to read.* Bethesda, MD: National Institute of Child Health and Human Development.

Institute for the Development of Educational Achievement (2002). *What are the Dynamic Indicators of Basic Early Literacy Skills or DIBELS?* Eugene, OR: University of Oregon.

Rasinski, T. V. (2004). *Assessing reading fluency.* Honolulu, HI: Pacific Resources for Education and Learning.

CHAPTER TEN

Teaching Comprehension

A s students with special needs in inclusive settings age, they are often still struggling readers and need additional support and help with both reading and writing. This chapter describes 22 ways struggling readers can be helped. Some of these ways are strategies that can be used to help struggling readers activate prior knowledge or more effectively and efficiently organize what they read. Others are actual approaches that can be used.

Strategies for Dealing with Prior Knowledge (Prereading Strategies)

1. K-W-L

K-W-L stands for *What we Know/What we want to Know/What we Learned.*

The Following steps can be used in implementing K-W-L:

a. Introduce the students to the K-W-L strategy with a new topic or text selection. If you choose a text selection, make sure it is nonfiction and deals with content with which students have at least some prior knowledge.

b. Have students tell what they think they know about the topic. (This is the K.)

c. Then write down the questions students have about the topic. (What do students want to know about the topic? This is the W.)

d. Have students read the text to answer the questions generated.

e. Have students revisit "what we know" to see if their knowledge was accurate.

f. See if the students' questions were answered from the "What we want to Know" chart.

g. Determine ways students can find the answers to their unanswered questions.

Adapted from Carr and Ogle (1987)

2. K-N-L

K-N-L stands for *What we Know/What we NEED to Know/What we Learned.* In the real world, there are times when students have to learn specific information. After determining the students' prior knowledge, you can then provide the objectives of what the students NEED to know. The procedure is the same as the K-W-L, but is more structured to prescribed objectives.

3. Mindset Approach

The mindset approach provides students with a perspective for reading.

Use the following steps when implementing the mindset approach.

a. Have a group of students read the same passage from two different perspectives. For example, have the students read a court case from a defendant's point of view or a prosecutor's perspective. A simpler example is to have one group of students re-read *The Three Little Pigs* from the pig's perspective and one group from the wolf's viewpoint.

b. Then, have the students discuss the passage from their given or chosen viewpoints.

Adapted from Pichert and Anderson (1977)

4. Prereading Plan (PreP)
PreP is a procedure to encourage group discussion and topic awareness.

The following steps can be used:
a. The teacher (or students) determine key terms
b. The teacher asks students to tell the associations or prior knowledge they have with the terms.
c. Then, the teacher fosters further discussion by asking, "Now that we have looked at these key terms, do you have any new ideas or questions before we read?"

Adapted from Langer (1981)

5. ReQuest
ReQuest stands for Reciprocal Questioning and involves student-teacher exchange and interaction to jumpstart reading.

The following steps can be used:
a. The teacher and students read the same segment or passage silently.

b. Students then question the teacher about the passage.

c. Next, the students and teacher change roles. The teacher asks students about what they've read.

d. Steps b. and c. are repeated.

e. After several interchanges, the teacher finally asks, "What do you think the rest of this passage is going to be about? Why? What made you decide that?"

f. Students then silently read the rest of the assignment.

g. A follow-up discussion is then conducted by the teacher or a student.

Adapted from Manzo and Manzo (1990)

6. Anticipation Guides

An anticipation guide is a group of statements. The students must individually respond to these before reading a passage, article, or chapter.

The following guidelines are recommended for developing an anticipation guide:

a. Decide the major ideas you want the students to glean from this passage.

b. Write these in short, declarative statements.

c. Put these statements in a format that will encourage the students to predict.

d. Discuss the students' predictions before they read the passage.

e. After students have read the selection, go back and compare the readers' predictions with the author's intended meaning.

Adapted from Manzo and Manzo (1990)

7. SQ3R

SQ3R stands for *Survey-Question-Read-Recite-Review.*

Use the following steps in implementing SQ3R:

a. Have students survey or notice the chapter titles and main headings and read the introductory and summary paragraphs. Point out the organization style, pictures, charts, graphs, and other visual aids at this time.

b. Have students question. Students are to turn the headings into questions.

c. Next, the students read to answer these questions.

d. Then, they *recite,* which simply means they answer the questions without looking back at the text.

e. Finally, students review by verifying their answers (that is, looking back at the text to see if they answered the questions correctly).

Adapted from Robinson (1970)

8. Guided Reading Procedures (GRP)

The Guided Reading Procedure can be used to improve students' organizational skills, comprehension, and recall.

The following steps are recommended:

a. Set a purpose for students reading a page or two of the passage or chapter.

b. Then have students close their books when they finish reading.

c. Students tell everything they have remembered from their reading while a teacher copies this on an overhead or chalk board.

d. Students are then directed to look at the selection again.

e. Students add to the list (on the overhead or board).

f. This procedure is repeated for the next section of the passage or chapter.

Adapted from Manzo and Manzo (1990)

9. Directed Inquiry Activity (DIA)

The Directed Inquiry Activity (DIA) is designed to help students set purposes for reading by constructing and answering questions about the passage.

The steps to the DIA include:

a. Have students invent questions about the passage using the following words: *who, what, when, where, how, how much, why,* and *which.*

b. Have students read to answer their questions.

c. Discuss their answers. For example, if the chapter or passage is about *Jamaica,* the students will invent one question for each word above. *Who lives in Jamaica? What is the capital of Jamaica?* Etc.

Adapted from Vacca and Vacca (1996)

Besides strategies that deal with prior knowledge at the beginning of reading, there are other ways to help students during and after they have read. Here are some of them.

10. REAP – Read-Encode-Annotate-Ponder

This strategy uses writing to improve thinking and reading.

The steps are:

a. **Read** to determine the author's message.

b. **Encode** the message by writing this in our own words.

c. **Annotate** by writing the message in notes for yourself or a thought book to share with other students.

d. **Ponder**, or reflect, on what you have read and written. First, do this individually. Then share this information with other students in a study session.

Adapted from Vacca and Vacca (1996)

11. Guided Lecture Procedure (GLP)

The Guided Lecture Procedure is a more teacher-directed method of improving listening during class.

The steps are:

a. Students are asked to take no notes as they listen carefully to the lecture.

b. The teacher writes the objectives for the lesson on the board or overhead along with key terms.
c. The teacher lectures for about half the class period and then stops.
d. Students are then directed to write down everything they recall from the lecture.
e. Students form small cooperative learning groups to review and discuss their notes, adding to each other's information.
f. Finally, the class discusses the information as a whole and the important points are reconstructed by the entire class.

Adapted from Kelly and Holmes (1979)

12. Webbing

Webbing is a graphic way to organize what one reads. A web can be constructed **before** students read, using their prior knowledge to construct the web. A web can also be used **during** reading to help students construct what they have learned up to that point. Finally, a web can be a great tool **after** reading to help students synthesize what they have read. An example of webbing completed on a social studies chapter on *Taiwan* is shown in Figure 10.1.

The steps are:
a. Students are directed to draw a circle in the middle of the paper.
b. Students then look for the main idea or topic idea in a paragraph, page, or chapter and write this in the center.

c. Students are then directed to look for related ideas and place these on the spokes of the web in a clockwise manner. This helps organize the ideas in order, particularly if there is a sequence to follow.

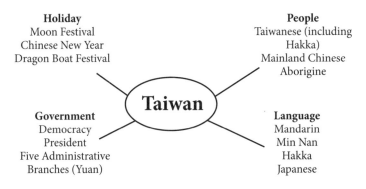

Holiday
Moon Festival
Chinese New Year
Dragon Boat Festival

People
Taiwanese (including Hakka)
Mainland Chinese
Aborigine

Taiwan

Government
Democracy
President
Five Administrative
Branches (Yuan)

Language
Mandarin
Min Nan
Hakka
Japanese

Figure 10.1   Web of social studies chapter on Taiwan

13. Pyramiding

Pyramiding is similar in structure to webbing. The only difference involves how ideas are shown graphically. Instead of organizing the material from the "inside-out" as done in webbing, pyramiding involves a "top-down" format. An example of pyramiding completed on the same social studies chapter from the webbing example is shown in Figure 10.2.

The steps are:

a. Students are directed to draw a square at the top of the paper.

b. Students look for the main idea or topic in a paragraph, page, or chapter and write this in the square at the top of the page.

c. Students are then directed to look for related

ideas and place these in squares below the main square at the top of the page.

d. Students then write sub-ideas under the squares and continue until all related ideas are exhausted.

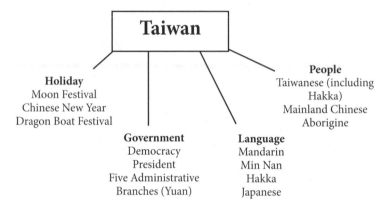

Figure 10.2   **Pyramid of a social studies chapter on Taiwan**

14. Think Sheets

Think Sheets are used before reading. They are purpose setters that are taken from chapter titles, heading, and subheadings. Think Sheets are used for students to predict what information may be in a section or chapter. They provide an excellent basis for discussing and sharing student viewpoints about the material to be learned.

The steps are:

a. The teacher chooses a specific chapter or section of a text that has subheadings.

b. The teacher writes all headings and subheadings on the board, an overhead, or a worksheet for the students. Space is left between each heading or subheading so that students can predict underneath each as to what that section might be about.

c. Students are directed to think about what information might be included under each subheading and discuss this with a partner.

d. Students then record their own predictions on their own paper.

e. Students then read the chapter to determine the accuracy of their own predictions.

f. Finally, the students meet with their original partners to see who predicted accurately and write down what information was actually in the text.

Adapted from Clewell and Haidemos (1983)

15. Discussion Webs

Discussion webs are used as a framework for students to explore passages and consider different viewpoints of an issue before drawing conclusions. A central question is posed in the center of the web that is primary to the reading of the passage. The question is written is such a way that it reflects more than just one viewpoint. Students consider the pros and cons of the question in "yes" and "no" columns of the web. Students meet in pairs and then in groups of four to discuss their answers. The four member team is asked to draw a conclusion based on their discussion of the web.

The steps are:

a. Students are prepared by the teacher for reading the text by activating the students' prior knowledge, asking questions, and creating predictions about the text.

b. Students read the selection and then the Discussion Web is introduced.

c. Students consider the pros and cons to the question. This is first done individually.

d. Then students meet in pairs to discuss their answers.

e. Students then meet in a group of four to continue discussing their answers.

f. The group of four is given three minutes to decide which of all the reasons given best supports the group's conclusions.

g. Students follow up with a whole-class discussion.

Adapted from Alverman (1991)

16. Text Rendering

Text rendering is a way to have students identify the most memorable features of a passage.

The steps are:

a. Students identify their most important sentence in a passage or chapter.

b. Students identify their most important phrase in the passage (which is NOT the same sentence as step a. above).

c. Students identify their most important word in a passage.

d. Students share their sentence, phrase, and word at the end of the lesson. Usually, students do not discuss these but simply read their passages.

Adapted from Pennsylvania State Department of Education

17. **I Wonder; Reminders; Questions for the Author**
    This procedure is designed to help students make
    meaningful connections with the text.

The steps are:
    a. Students write down what they are curious about
       (after reading the passage).
    b. Students write down things of which this passage
       reminds them.
    c. Students then write down questions they would
       like to ask the author about the passage.

Adapted from Cleaveland and Ray (2004)

18. **Double Entry Journals**
    Double Entry Journals are designed for students
    to summarize what they are learning and then to
    personally comment on it.

The steps are:
    a. Students divide a journal page in half by either
       drawing a line down the middle of the page

       similar to a steno notebook or folding the page
       length-wise in half.
    b. Students write summary statements of what they
       are learning on the left hand side of the sheet.
    c. Students write their reflections, reactions, or
       questions on the right hand side.
    d. Students discuss their Double Entry Journals in
       groups or with the teacher. Whole class discus-
       sions are also encouraged.

Adapted from Vacca and Vacca (1996)

19. Venn Diagrams

Venn diagrams are designed to help students compare and contrast two texts or two ideas that are similar but also different in some ways.

The steps are:

a. The teacher draws two overlapping circles.
b. Ideas that are common to both texts are placed in the center.
c. Ideas that are specific to one of the texts or ideas are placed in the outer section of the circles.

An example of a Venn diagram comparing Philadelphia with New York City is shown in Figure 10.3.

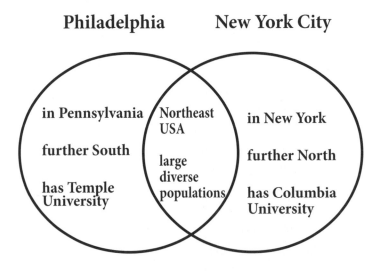

Figure 10.3   Venn Diagram

S ometimes more than two ideas or texts can be compared. Sometime three or four ideas need to be compared and contrasted. In the case of three ideas or texts, a triangle can be used for comparison. The triangle adds a new dimension. Ideas that are common to two of the texts/ideas can be shown outside the triangle. An example of a triangle variation on a Venn diagram is shown in Figure 10.4. In this example, similarities and differences among Philadelphia, New York City, and Washington DC are shown. Ideas that are unique to one city are found in the smaller, outer triangles, and finally, ideas that are similar in only tow of the cities are listed outside the triangle.

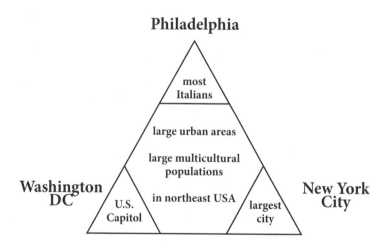

Figure 10.4   Triangular variation of a Venn Diagram

In the case of four ideas that are compared and contrasted, a "house" can be sued for this comparison. The concepts that are alike will go in the "roof" or triangle at the top. The ideas that are unique to each will go in the assigned square. Figure 10.5 shows the similarities and differences among Philadelphia, New York City, Washington DC, and Boston.

Adapted from Miller (2002)

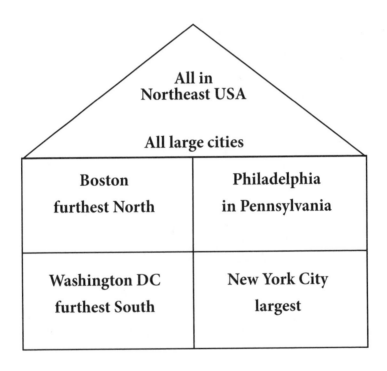

Figure 10.5   **"House" variation of a Venn Diagram**

20. The Fernald Approach/Modified – The V.A.K.T. Approach

Grace Fernald (1943) developed a multisensory approach to teaching reading and writing many years ago. The approach incorporated the sensory input of visual, auditory, kinesthetic, and tactile modes.

The following steps are to be done with an individual child. However, the procedure can be adapted to use with a small group of students.

a. The student tells a story.

b. The teacher writes the story on large cards or in a notebook.

c. The child is asked to read the story back to the teacher.

d. The teacher makes note of words the student misses while the child reads.

e. The teach rewrites or prints each word missed in large letters on a sentence strip or index card.

f. The teacher pronounces the word for the child and then the child is asked to trace the word with the index finger while saying each letter as he completes it. The child then says the whole word after he completes this.

g. The child repeats tracing and saying the letters of the word until he believes he can print or write the word from memory.

h. The student then writes the word from memory on another sheet of paper.

i. If the child writes the word correctly without stopping, the next word is taught, using the same method.

j. If the child writes the word incorrectly or pauses

too long in writing, the student is asked to trace the word until he is ready to write the word quickly from memory.

k. The teacher continues teaching the words missed until all the words are learned.

l. The words are then filed in an index card box.

m. The story is filed in the back of the box.

n. Before the next lesson, the teacher types the story.

o. At the beginning of the next lesson, the teachers asks the child to read the typed story.

p. The teacher reteaches any words missed by using the tracing method above.

q. Handwriting and spelling can also be taught using the words.

Adapted from Fernald (1943)

21. The Writing Process for Older Struggling Readers
In Chapter Two we described the beginnings of the writing process. We called this "Draw and Write". When children reach approximately second grade and above, they are introduced to the writing process for older students. For a detailed description of the writing process see Graves (1983). Listed below are the steps used in the Writing Process for older students.

Steps in the Writing Process

a. Rehearsing. This is more commonly known as brainstorming. Students are asked to write down ideas they might have for writing a story. Story starters are not recommended. Each student has something to write about without a prompt. If a student cannot think of anything to write about, then that student is directed to look at his or her journal to see if any ideas emerge.

b. Drafting. At this stage students write down their ideas for a story. The purpose here is to get the ideas down on paper. Students will eventually have at least two or three drafts.

c. Revising. At this stage students begin revising their stories by looking at the sequence, if their stories make sense, if they are communicating what they wished. Revisions are important, and this step usually spills over to the editing stage.

d. Editing. At the editing stage the students attend to grammar, spelling, and story structure and move toward editing their stories into a final form. The teacher serves as the final editor, assisting students in making the final changes that will reflect the students' best work.

e. Publishing. Finally, students' stories are published when their stories have been through the final editing stage. Stories are to be bound into a "real book". Publishing provides a real world reason for students to write and edit their stories. These stories can become a part of the classroom library.

Adapted from Graves (1983)

The writing process usually occurs during writing workshop. The writing workshop should be structured so that the students will know what is expected of them and so they can work in an environment in which they know the rules. Listed below are suggestions from the writing workshop that were adapted from Gurosky (1986).

a. The writing workshop should occur at a set time every day. This could be from 35 minutes to one hour, depending on the students and curriculum restrictions.

b. Students work at their own pace through the writing process so there is no waiting for other students to catch up or to slow down.

c. When a student finishes one story, after the final editing process, he begins another story. Every child is at one of the steps in the writing process described by Graves (1983) but not at the same place as other students.

d. Each student is assigned a specific day for conferencing. If a child needs help on a day that he is not scheduled for conferencing, he may put his name on the board for teacher help or ask another student for help through peer conferencing.

e. Each child has two folders. One folder is kept at the writing center or by the child to work on each day. The second folder is kept by the teacher and contains the final, edited work of that student.

f. In the folder that the teacher keeps, the student's

strengths are written on the left inside section of the folder. The right inside section contains suggestions for improving the child's writing. These are discussed and refined during the teacher/child conference time.

g. The rehearsing, drafting, revising, and editing steps of the writing process occur the first three weeks of every month. The last week of each month is used for publishing week. Each student must publish a book that week. At the end of the school year each child will have published a minimum of nine books.

h. There are definitely no story starters used. Children always choose what they will write about. The teacher models how students can choose something to write about.

i. A mini-lesson is usually taught the first five minutes of the period.

j. Sharing time occurs during the last five minutes of the period, with those who had conferences that day receiving priority for sharing.

Adapted from Gurosky (1986)

22. Self-Evaluation on Writing and Examinations

All students need to practice self-evaluation. This gives them an opportunity to report what they think they missed or misspelled.

The steps are:

a. After a test, have students write what they believe they missed on the test and why.

b. Have students also do this with their spelling, grammar, and word problems on mathematics tests.

c. Students who are not good at judging their mistakes can be helped through scaffolding by the teacher. For example, if the child does not believe he misspelled any words, the teacher can say, "Look at this line. You have two misspelled words on this line. Can you find them?"

This chapter considered 22 ways to improve reading and writing for older struggling readers. These strategies, approaches, or activities are appropriate for all students but are vital for students who need extra help and support. While all of these methods are salient and appropriate, we must note that they are mostly teacher-directed and teacher-imposed on the students. The teacher will not always be around to assist struggling readers and writers. Therefore, students must be taught ways to monitor their own learning and comprehension.

All of the strategies we have discussed up to this point are externally imposed by the teacher. However, students need to be taught strategies to *internally* monitor their own reading. If we help them do this, then they can use these the rest of their lives. This section is concerned with seven metacognitive strategies that should be taught to all children from kindergarten through graduate school. However, it is recommended that a teacher focus on just one at a time and work with students on this one for a period of five to six weeks before moving to another strategy.

These seven strategies are based on a synthesis of research on what good readers do when they read. While these seven strategies were researched some 20 years ago, it was not until Keene and Zimmerman (1997) and Miller (2002) wrote about how to apply these in the classroom that these strategies became important in classrooms. For a thorough understanding of these strategies we recommend the above mentioned texts as necessary reading.

Every time the teacher teaches a new strategy, she models this for the students. She shows them how she activates this strategy when she reads. Remember, each strategy should be taught for five to six weeks before moving to another strategy. The reason for this is so that students will automatically make this a part of their reading when they read. Strategies do not have to be taught in a particular order.

Activating Prior Knowledge (Schema) (Anderson & Person, 1984)

Activating prior knowledge is useful in helping with recall. The teacher models schema in the following ways. She says the following when she is reading aloud to the students, reminding them she is using schema.

"This reminds me of…"

"I thought about this when I read this passage…"

"This made me think of…"

"I read something else that said this…"

The teacher uses text-to-self connections as she states what the passage reminded her of in terms of her personal life. The teacher also uses text-to-text connections. The teacher says, "That reminded me of a passage in another book we read." The teacher also models text-to-world connections in which she points out how things in the book connect to the world outside.

Determining Importance (Palinscar & Brown, 1984)

Determining importance helps children focus. Students are taught to notice what they believe is most important about the author's message. Children must defend their positions and give reasons they have determined what they believe is important. Children are also taught to determine a few key themes. The teacher models by using some of the following statements.

"Based on what I know, I think this is important…"

"From what I have read up until now, I think that this important…"

"The most important thing to me is…"

Questioning (Raphael, 1984)

Children are taught to ask questions of themselves, the authors, and the texts they read. Students are told to ask questions before, during, and after reading. The teacher encourages students by asking questions such as, "What are you wondering about?" "What are you confused about?" "Why?" Asking questions helps students clarify what they are reading.

Creating Mental Images (Visual or Other Sensory Images) (Pressley, 1976)

Here, the teacher models what she is picturing when she reads. What are the smells, tastes, or sounds she imagines when she reads this passage? Mental images are important to deepen our understanding of the text. Some of the things a teacher might say to model visual, auditory, or other sensory connections include:

"I pictured this when I read…What did you picture?"

"I could hear the person talking in this passage…"

"I could smell the cakes the woman was baking. They smelled like the cakes my grandmother used to make."

Inferring (Hansen, 1981)

To infer is to go beyond the literal meaning and open the world of meaning connected to our situations. Predictions are the beginning of inference. What is implied is not always written in the text. Also, drawing inferences helps us make critical judgments and make unusual or imaginative interpretations. Teachers can model inferring by saying some of the following when reading aloud to students.

"I really appreciated how…"

"I will guess that…"

"What I didn't like was…"

"I think the following is going to happen…"

Synthesis (Miller, 2002)

Good readers know when they are not getting it. Teachers can model ways that good readers monitor what they are reading. This helps readers become more independent and use "fix-up" strategies when comprehension breaks down. The teacher can model monitoring for comprehension by using some of the following statements.

"I read this part again because…"

"I had trouble with this part of the text because…"

Note: many of the examples for teaching the seven metacognitive strategies for comprehension were adapted from Keene & Zimmerman (1997) and Miller (2002).

Summary

Good readers automatically use these seven strategies when they read. Reading is social knowledge, and students, particularly those with reading difficulties, cannot be expected to pick these up on their own. Explicit instruction on each of the seven strategies is usually necessary to ensure comprehension.

Many teachers realize that teaching phonics in some format is necessary for students to understand and identify the 44 sounds of the English language. However, many do not realize that comprehension does not automatically result when a student is able to pronounce words. Explicit teaching of comprehension is also necessary. These seven strategies can be used to do just that.

REFERENCES

Alvermann, D.E. (1991). The discussion web: A graphic aid for learning across the curriculum. *The Reading Teacher,* 45(2), 92-99.

Anderson, R., & Pearson, P.D. (1984). A schema-theoretic view of basic processes in reading. In *Handbook of Reading Research,* P.D. Pearson (ed.). White Plains, NY: Longman.

Brown, A., Day, J., & Jones, E. (1983). The development of plans for summarizing texts. *Child Development,* 54, 968-979.

Carr, E. & Ogle, D. (1987). K-W-L Plus: A strategy for comprehension and summarization, *Journal of Reading,* 20, 626-631.

Cleaveland, L., and Ray, K.W. (2004). *Writing workshop with our youngest writers.* Portsmouth, NH: Heinemann.

Clewell, S., & Haidemos, J. (1983). Organizational strategies to increase comprehension. *Reading World,* 22(4), 314-321.

Fernald, G.M. (1943). *Remedial techniques in basic school subjects.* New York, McGraw-Hill.

Graves, D. (1983). *Writing: Teachers and children at work.* Portsmouth, NH: Heinemann.

Gurosky, L. (1986, November). *A second grader's revision: One part of the writing process.* Paper presented at the 15th annual meeting of the Mid-South Educational Research Association, Memphis, TN.

Hansen, J. (1981). The effects of inference training and practice on young children's reading comprehension. *Reading Research Quarterly,* 16, 391-417.

Keene, E., & Zimmerman, S. (1997). *Mosaic of thought: Teaching comprehension in a reader's workshop.* Portsmouth, NH: Heinemann.

Kelly, B.. & Holmes, J. (1979). The guided lecture procedures, *Journal of Reading,* 22, 602-604.

Langer, J. (1981), November). From theory to practice: A prereading plan. *Journal of Reading,* 25, 152-156.

Manzo, A., & Manzo, U. (1990). *Content area reading: A heuristic approach.* Columbus, OH: Charles E. Merrill.

Miller, D. (2002). *Reading with meaning.* Portland, ME: Stenhouse.

Palinscar, A. & Brown, A. (1984). Reciprocal teaching of comprehension fostering and monitoring activities. *Cognition and Instruction,* 1, 117-175.

Pichert, J., & Anderson, R. (1977). Taking different perspectives on a story. *Journal of Educational Psychology,* 69, 309-315.

Pressley, G. (1976). Mental imagery helps eight-year-olds remember what they read. *Journal of Educational Psychology,* 68, 355-359.

Raphael, T. (1984). Teaching learners about sources of information for answering questions. *Journal of Reading,* 27, 303-311.

Robinson, F.P. (1970). *Effective Study* (4th Ed). New York: Harper & Row.

Vacca, R., & Vacca, J. (1996). *Content area reading.* New York: HarperCollins.

EPILOGUE

This source has been concerned with an understanding of what literacy means in the 21st century, what it means to be reading and writing, and how to teach struggling readers in the beginning as well as the more advanced stages of literacy.

While all students can benefit from the strategies, activities, and methods described here, we are most concerned with literacy instruction for students with special needs in the coming months and years. The reauthorization of Title I and IDEA present new challenges for teachers and students in inclusive settings. Students in special education are now being tested with their regular education peers and what used to be considered an established disability is now in question due to changes in IDEA. Still, good instruction is necessary and important for all the students we serve. We hope this resource will help you meet the challenges of teaching literacy in inclusive settings.

Renitta Goldman, Ph.D., is a Professor of Special Education at the University of Alabama at Birmingham. She is the author of several books and articles. On several occasions Dr. Goldman has been invited to present papers at international conferences. She is Principal Investigator of two four-year federally funded training grants and has been a grant reviewer for several federal agencies. She served many years in the public schools as well as in higher education. She has a long-term role as coordinator of UAB's Special Education programs. Her professional interests include assessment and the prevention of child abuse.

Jerry Aldridge, Ed.D., is a Professor of Early Childhood Education at the University of Alabama at Birmingham. He is editor of Focus on Inclusive Education and also for Among the Periodicals for the Association for Childhood Education International. He is a former president of the United States National Committee for the World Organization for Early Childhood Education (OMEP). He has been quoted in Parenting Magazine, The Chicago Sun Times, USA Today, and has appeared on the Health News Network and CNN Headline News.

Kelly A. Russell, M.A.Ed., is a doctoral student and teaching and research assistant at the University of Alabama at Birmingham. She has served as adjunct faculty at UAB and Athens State University. She has worked for more than 10 years in early childhood education classrooms and has served as a literacy coach with an Early Reading First grant project. Ms. Russell has presented at regional, national, and international conferences and has numerous publications to her credit.

NOTES